COLORS OF

Mexico

AA Publishing

Author: Mona King

Produced by AA Publishing

Published by AA Publishing (a trading name of Automobile Association Developments Limited, whose registered office is Fanum House, Basing View, Basingstoke, Hampshire RG21 4EA; registered number 1878835)

ISBN-10: 0-7495-4670-0
ISBN-13: 978-0-7495-4670-0

A02530

A CIP catalogue record for this book is available from the British Library.

Layouts by Andrew Milne Design
Printed and bound in China

COLORS OF

Mexico

CONT

1
FLAVORS

2
LIFE & PEOPLE

3
ARCHITECTURE

INTRODUCTION 6

CREDITS 144

TORTILLAS 20

TEQUILA 24

FRUIT MARKETS 26

AGUA 28

CHOCOLATE
& CHILI 30

RELIGION 36

LIFE IN THE
ZOCALO 38

COSTUME 40

CHARROS 46

TRADITIONAL
CRAFTS 48

LEISURE TIME 52

HIGH FLYERS 54

PYRAMIDS 58

CHURCHES 60

A PLACE
TO REFLECT 64

MODERN DESIGN 66

BOLD FACADES 72

FRENCH STYLE 74

COLONIAL 76

COLORS OF **MEXICO**

4
LANDMARKS & VIEWS

LA BANDERA 80

MEXICO CITY 82

PILLARS & TEMPLES 86

VOLCANOES 88

DESERT CACTI 90

TROPICAL FLOWERS 92

5
ART, CULTURE & STYLE

COLOSSAL SCULPTURES 98

THE MURALISTS 100

PAINTING 102

CARVINGS 104

ANCIENT RITUALS 106

MUSIC OF MEXICO 108

6
LIGHT & REFLECTIONS

UNDERWATER WORLD 114

WATERFALLS 118

CAVERNS 120

STAINED GLASS 122

NIGHTLIFE 124

7
TIME & MOTION

ON THE MOVE 130

TO COPPER CANYON 132

OPEN ROAD 134

DAWN & DUSK 136

SURFING THE WAVES 138

DIA DE LOS MUERTOS 142

INTROD

To visit Mexico is to enter a whole new world. One which can seduce, intrigue, bewilder, and totally captivate you. A veritable kaleidoscope of images, landscapes, flavors and aromas, culture and art, it reaches out to all the senses. Throughout the country there is an all-pervading sense of light and color, from its decorative murals, colorful handicrafts, displays of tropical market fruits, to brilliant blossoms and flowering trees, accentuated by the luminosity of its skies.

From its extensive northern border with the United States, Mexico curves southward in a distinctive horn shape to the Central American countries of Guatemala and Belize, with the long finger of Baja California jutting down from southern California into the Pacific Ocean. The two great mountain ranges of the Sierra Madre Occidental and the Sierra Madre Oriental which sweep down western and eastern Mexico, have endowed the country with scenery of wild, stunning beauty, dominated by mighty canyons, plunging gorges, and deep valleys. Cacti-studded deserts in the north contrast with its central plateau, a region characterized by lakes, fresh alpine scenery, and spectacular snow-capped volcanoes. Dense tropical rainforests in the south give way to the flat limestone shelf of the Yucatan peninsula in the east. A long coastline of almost six thousand miles borders the Gulf of California and the Pacific Ocean to the west, while its eastern shores are washed by the Gulf of Mexico and the Caribbean.

While Mexico ranks as a modern developing nation, it is also a country whose present is closely interwoven with its ancient roots. And whichever way you turn you will find yourself surrounded by reminders of the past; not only in the pyramids and temples of pre-Hispanic times, the baroque churches, colonial cities, and splendid museums, but in the living evidence of the descendants of these former civilizations: the indigenous population, whose way of life has changed little over the centuries. Throughout the country you have only to visit the marketplace, a fiesta, or merely walk through the streets, to find yourself among the local people dressed in their colorful, traditional garments, going about their business and communicating in their own language.

These dramatic contrasts and sharp extremes between such varying lifestyles are all part of the intricate pattern of today's Mexico. In reality there are many Mexicos. While sometimes hard to grasp the complexities, mysteries, and paradoxes of this extraordinary land, it is rare to remain indifferent to it.

Archaeological treasures

Numerous archaeological sites remain as a lasting legacy of the succession of cultures that rose and fell, long before the arrival of the Spaniards in 1517. To explore some of these ancient ruins is a wonderful way of learning about the country's enigmatic past, and most of its major sites are easily accessible from main centers.

The earliest of the developed civilizations were known as the Olmecs. They flourished in the coastal regions of Veracruz and Tabasco between c. 1200 and 500 BC, where they sculpted extraordinary colossal heads with Negroid features. These, and other sculptures, can be seen in the excellent Museums of Anthropology in Mexico City and Xalapa, in addition to the well-presented open-air Parque Museo La Venta in Villahermosa.

The following Classic period, c. AD 250–900, saw the growth of other civilizations. Dominant centers were those of the Zapotecs at Monte Albán in Oaxaca, El Tajín (the Totonac capital), and Teotihuacán, northeast of Mexico City. The greatest of all the pre-Hispanic cultures, however, is thought to be that of the Maya. Spread over Chiapas, the Yucatan peninsula, and part of Central America, the Maya reached great heights in the spheres of architecture, astronomy, and mathematical calculations. Chichén Itzá and Uxmal in the Yucatan and Palenque, in Chiapas, are among the most important of the ancient Mayan sites that have been excavated and well restored.

As successive civilizations collapsed, new cultures emerged. The Mixtecs took over Monte Albán and Mitla, while to the north of Mexico City, the Toltecs built their capital at Tula. From here their legendary leader Quetzalcóatl, the Plumed Serpent, is said to have departed for the Yucatan, but with the prediction that he would return.

By the time the Mexica (later called the Aztecs) appeared in the Valley of Mexico most of these civilizations had gone into decline and their once great centers had been abandoned. From the founding of their capital Tenochtitlán on Lake Texcoco, up until the arrival in 1519 of Hernán Cortés and his band of soldiers, the Aztecs built up a mighty empire. Emperor Moctezuma´s belief that Cortés was the famous Quetzalcóatl returnng from the east, as foretold, plus the support Cortés received from some of the Indian tribes, who were hostile to the Aztecs, played a significant role in the ensuing events. A final battle in 1521 saw the total destruction of Tenochtitlán and the subsequent demise of the Aztec civilization.

As a result, relatively little has remained of Mexico´s last great pre-Hispanic culture. Traces of the former Templo Mayor (Great Temple), uncovered in recent years, can be seen just off Mexico City´s Zócalo (the city's main plaza, on the site of the old Aztec city square), along with a museum depicting the lives of the Aztecs. A number of impressive sculptures and artefacts are displayed in the Mexica Hall of the city's National Museum of Anthropology, and there are a few small Aztec sites in the area surrounding Mexico City.

Birth of a new nation

The Spaniards established their rule over "New Spain" as they called their colony, beginning by building its new capital city over the ruins of the former Aztec city of Tenochtitlán. The arrival of the Spanish changed the course of history. During their three hundred years of colonialism, the

Spaniards introduced their own cultures to Mexico, in the form of religion, language, customs, and architecture. They founded and developed new towns, and built fine mansions, palaces, and magnificent churches, cathedrals, and monasteries across the entire country. Among the most charming of these Spanish colonial towns are Morelia, Guanajuato, San Miguel de Allende, Oaxaca, Puebla, and Taxco.

The fusion of the Spaniards and Indians produced a significant new race, that of the mestizo, which denotes a person of mixed race. Today, the vast majority of Mexico's population is made up of mestizos, with the indigenous races representing some 15 percent or so of the total.

Independence from Spanish rule in 1821 was followed by a long period of instability and turmoil; war with the United States, the ceding of a great chunk of its former territories, the French intervention, and the 1864–67 fateful rule of Hapsburg Emperor Maximilian. After the turbulence and chaos of the 1910–20 Revolution, calm and order gradually returned to the country. The second half of the twentieth century saw the modernization and industrialization of Mexico, mainly concentrated on the capital.

The modern era has brought about peace and progress and the use of natural assets to cater for new demands. Not the least of these has been the growth of tourism and the inevitable development of beach resorts. If your idea of heaven is sunshine, sea, and a glorious palm-fringed beach, you will surely find it here in Mexico.

Resorts

Both the Pacific and Caribbean coasts offer an abundance of vacation spots, each with its own distinctive personality. The famous Pacific resort of Acapulco needs no introduction. From its early days in the 1920s it long reigned supreme as Mexico's best-known destination. With its string of high-rise deluxe hotels and swimming pools lining Acapulco Bay, a breathtaking sight day or night, it still holds on to its reputation. But a whole host of other resorts have since appeared on the scene, with development ever on the increase.

You can choose from Zihuatanejo, Puerto Vallarta, Mazatlán, the newer resorts of Ixtapa, Los Cabos, and Huatulco, or you might like to settle for any one of the exotic hotel complexes dotted along the coastline.

White sandy beaches, clear turquoise waters, and some spectacular scuba diving characterize Mexico's Caribbean coast. Star resort has to be Cancún which offers all the facilities holidaymakers come to expect from a top beach destination, in addition to serving as a convenient gateway to the Mayan ruins. To the south is the fast growing Riviera Maya, with an increasing number of complexes and hotels stretching way down the coast; while across the waters the small islands of Cozumel and Isla Mujeres have long been popular centers.

A performer entertaining at the tourist resort of La Bufadora (right).
Next page: The coast at San José del Cabo, at the tip of the Baja California peninsula.

Adventure travel

Mexico has a multitude of other riches besides beaches and can offer unique experiences to the adventurous traveler who wants to explore the country. Ride the Chihuahua al Pacifico railway through the spectacular Copper Canyon; visit the Monarch butterfly sanctuary in Michoacán to marvel at the butterflies that flock there in their millions; join an expedition on the Usamacinta river in southern Chiapas, to visit the remote archaeological sites of Bonampak, Yaxchilán, and Piedras Negras, or enter the silent, mystical world of the multi-hued lagoons of Monte Bello.

In the Yucatán you can explore fascinating caves or *cenotes* (sinkholes) of great natural beauty, where you can swim, dive, or merely relax and enjoy the view. Wildlife enthusiasts will appreciate the colonies of pink flamingos at the Río Lagartos National Park, or the Celestún Wildlife Refuge, on the Yucatán's northern shores. In many parts of the country there are opportunities for hiking, climbing, horseback riding, and rafting.

Worlds apart is Baja California, Mexico's "last vacation frontier." A drive down through some of the peninsula's remoter parts can prove to be quite a challenge, taking you through some bizarre landscapes of lunarlike deserts and towering cacti. Here, a pioneering spirit and a suitable high-clearance vehicle are absolute essentials for enjoying the trip.

In the early part of the year you can visit the sanctuaries of Ojo de Liebre, San Ignacio, or Bahía Magdalena, on the Pacific side of the peninsula, to watch the extraordinary spectacle of the grey whales that arrive annually from Alaska in their thousands to mate and calve. You will also come across excellent facilities for deep-sea fishing.

Remember that life in Mexico can be totally unpredictable. However this very element of the unknown is part of the Mexican experience and adds a certain spice to traveling. Frustrations can be offset by pleasant surprises of a most unusual nature, so that you instantly forget any annoyances. Always expect the unexpected and be prepared for any eventuality.

Mexican hospitality

It is the Mexican people themselves who form the real heart and soul of the country. To have good friends among them, to spend time with them, will open your eyes to another side of Mexico, adding a totally new dimension to your understanding of the country.

While the Mexican's initial attitude is generally one of warmth and friendliness, a meaningful friendship may well take time to develop. Once close bonds have been established, however, your host's kindness and generosity knows no boundaries. Mexican hospitality is legendary and can be quite overwhelming. When taken under someone's wing you will be shown around, introduced to their friends, accepted instantly, and feel totally protected.

While Mexicans generally prefer to entertain out, a firmly forged friendship can lead to an invitation to the family home—something of an honor. An extra guest, even if unexpected, is never a problem, with room enough, ample food and drink, and a warm welcome from all present. Be prepared for anything. An initial invitation to lunch can turn into a party, with a continuous flow of relatives and friends coming and going until the early hours of the following morning.

Out in the countryside entertainment is on a lavish scale. An invitation to one of the ranches in central or northern Mexico, to experience a lively local *charreada* or rodeo will give you an insight into another sort of Mexican lifestyle, unknown to most visitors. A new face can spark off great interest: be ready for further invitations and some hectic ranch hopping.

You can leave Mexico with so many lasting impressions; sunset over Acapulco, snow-capped volcanoes, the jungle ruins of Palenque, whale watching in San Ignacio lagoon, a Tarahumara Indian poised on the ridge of a canyon, a smiling Maya woman in her embroidered *huipil*. But hardest to beat is the simple memory of good times spent with Mexican friends, talking, laughing, and sharing jokes, leaving you with a warm feeling of welcome and an understanding of the Mexican way of life—and a yearning to return to this wonderful and unique land.

Next page: The road between Hidalgo del Parral and Durango runs dead straight for miles across the Alto Plano.

TORTILLAS 20

TEQUILA 24

MARKETS 26

COLORS OF MEXICO: **FLAVORS**

CHOCOLATE & CHILI 30

AGUA 28

Mexico is a feast for the eyes, the nose, the tastebuds. The intensity of color in fruit and vegetable markets is an experience in itself, while the aromas of tacos, grilled corn, pork, or chicken drifting from street vendors' stalls exude a unique flavor of Mexico.

When the Spaniards arrived in Mexico they discovered a diet based on corn, beans, chilli peppers, vanilla, herbs, potatoes, cacao beans, tropical fruit, wild game, and fish. They in turn introduced chicken, pigs, goats, cheese, nuts, garlic, and sugar to the New World. While Mexican cuisine has been subject to European influences over the years, it retains its own totally distinctive and unmistakable flavor, with each region offering its own particular specialties. There is grilled *cabrito* (baby goat) from Monterrey, *mole poblano* (chilli, nut, and chocolate sauce) from Puebla, fresh seafood from the Gulf Coast, and *cochinita pibil* (a spiced pork dish) from the Yucatan, and many more tasty dishes to be enjoyed. But wherever you go, you will find basic Mexican cooking revolves around tortillas, *refritos* (refried beans), avocados, and chillies.

The tortilla is a flat pancake made from corn, the staple diet of the native people centuries ago. While increasingly produced by modern presses, you will still see local Indian women making tortillas in the traditional way, patting them patiently by hand, one by one, until wafer thin.

Numerous dishes are formed around the tortilla. On its own, it fulfils the function of bread. Filled with beef, chicken, pork, or other ingredients, it becomes a taco, with many tasty variants such as quesadillas, enchiladas, burritos, and tostadas.

Wherever you are in Mexico you need not worry about going hungry or thirsty. Tempting tacos and countless tortilla-based snacks are available from street vendors in towns, while fruits, sweets, and cooling juices are always on offer from beach vendors roaming the popular resorts.

TEQUILA

The popularity of tequila, Mexico's fiery national drink, knows no bounds, finding its place among familiar bottles in well-stocked bars the world over. The famous margarita, combining tequila, Triple Sec and lime juice, has become a firm favorite among cocktail drinkers, with the tequila sunrise following closely in its wake. However there are numerous other concoctions waiting to be discovered, depending on your personal taste. Many Mexicans prefer to drink tequila neat, with a lick of salt and a suck of lime, or with a shot of spiced tomato and orange, known as a sangrita.

Tequila is produced from the *Agave tequiliana* plant, which grows in the areas around the town of Tequila, near Guadalajara. The brew is made by fermenting the roasted heart of the agave and distilling the resulting liquid twice, before ageing it in wooden casks.

Mexico's long tradition of buying and selling at the marketplace continues today, principally among the indigenous people, with each town and village holding at least one weekly market. Exotic aromas waft from great piles of chillis, spices, and herbs, while vast arrays of vegetables and exotic fruits add brilliant color to the scene. Whether wandering around the market or taking your pick at a hotel breakfast table, the choice of fruit is enormous. Among the abundance of fruit produced in Mexico you will find oranges, pineapples, melons and water melons, papayas, mangoes, avocados, sapodillas (prickly pears), guava, mamey (a type of mangosteen) and limes, which are popularly squeezed over other fruits to add zest.

FRUIT MARKETS

AGUA

Although perhaps better known for its more exotic cocktails and fresh fruit juices, Mexico produces some excellent mineral water. The quiet little spa town of Tehuacán, southeast of Puebla, is known for supplying most of the bottled water consumed throughout the country.

The healing powers of thermal springs were recognized by the Aztecs: Emperor Moctezuma is known to have visited them. Attractive spa resorts offering health treatments have been developed around a number of thermal springs, mainly in the central heartlands of the country.

The combination of chocolate and hot chili peppers that originates in Mexico, may seem an unlikely one, but it is no joke. One of Emperor Moctezuma's favorite beverages was chocolate (from Xocolatl, in the Aztec language of Nahuatl), made from cacao beans and with hot chili peppers, vanilla, and herbs added to the foaming brew. Hot chocolate later became a fashionable drink in European society and is just as popular today with both adults and children. The cacao bean (from the pod, far right) was also used as a form of currency by the Aztecs and other tribes.

At least a hundred varieties of chilies are grown in Mexico, but the jalapeño pepper is one of the most popular and frequently encountered. Chillies are used in many different dishes, each with its own distinctive regional flavor. Mexico's national dish, *mole poblano*, originally developed by the nuns of

CHOCOLATE & CHILI

Puebla, is centered around turkey or chicken served
in a rich dark sauce, whose ingredients include
chillies and bitter chocolate.
Next page: Benito Juarez market in Oaxaca.

LIFE & PEOPLE

RELIGION 36

ZOCALO 38

COSTUME 40

CHARROS 46

TRADITIONAL CRAFTS 48

HIGH FLYERS 54

LEISURE TIME 52

RELIGION

Mexico is a land of many peoples, with a strong and very visible divide between the mestizos, of mixed ancestry, and the indigenous people, who have maintained their ethnic identity. The typical Mexican tends to be genial, outgoing, generous, hospitable, and charming, with a strong feeling of nationalism and a sense of pride in his or her heritage. He or she also has great humor and a capacity for shrugging off problems and enjoying life, and has seemingly little in common with a fellow Indian from a poor rural region. However he or she will have inherited characteristics from Indian forefathers, such as stoicism, patience, courtesy, and a certain fatalism. Similar characteristics are still seen among indigenous peoples today. In addition, they are humble, modest, and possess great dignity. Silent by nature, they prefer to keep to themselves and, while mostly welcoming to visitors, some groups can be mistrustful of strangers.

After the conquest a succession of missionaries sent over from Spain set about converting the native Indians to Christianity by incorporating Christianity into pre-Hispanic religions. Catholicism in Mexico today is still interwoven with ancient native beliefs, clearly portrayed in local celebrations and fiestas.

The legend of the appearance of the Virgin of Guadalupe (right) to the Indian Juan Diego in 1531was a significant factor in acceptance of the Catholic religion. The dark-skinned Virgin is revered as Mexico's patron and the Basilica of Guadalupe is an important pilgrimage site.

Focal point of any town or village is the main plaza, popularly known as the zócalo. These delightful squares, usually dominated by the cathedral or parish church and with portales (arcades), neatly trimmed trees, fountains and benches, are a gathering place for local people.

ZOCALO

Open-air cafés are a good place to observe the activities taking place in the livelier plazas. Balloon and flower sellers, and shoeshiners are a familiar sight, amidst vendors vying to sell their wares, in and out of the arcades, with roving musicians and bandstand concerts adding to the entertainment.

COSTUME

When traveling around you will be struck by the striking colors and sheer diversity of the traditional Indian costumes which are still worn in many parts of the country. Some of the most colorful costumes can be seen in the states of Oaxaca, Veracruz and the Yucatan, where the Mayan women dressed in their delightful embroidered huipils are a familiar part of the scene.

Ethnic groups in the highlands of Chiapas are renowned for their colorful attire, which varies from one village to another. Flat straw hats adorned with brightly colored tassels are widely seen among the menfolk, while the women go about their daily business in richly embroidered blouses worn over a woven skirt (above).

The main square (or *zócalo*) in any town or village is still the heart of the community and a regular meeting place. Here, occupying benches or gathered in small groups exchanging news, is the familiar sight of local menfolk in their panama hats—practically a uniform in many regions.

Panama hats have been produced in Becal, Campeche, since the middle of the nineteenth century. These soft hats are woven mainly by women who work making the hats in limestone caves all over town. Here the humidity is just the right level to keep the fibers of the jipi palms moist and pliable. Connoisseurs claim that the test of a true panama hat is to crumple it into a ball, pass it through a ring, and shake it out again to its original shape.

Next page: Traditionally decorated sombreros.

CHARROS

Horses were introduced to Mexico by the Spanish
conquistadores, initially terrifying the local Indians
who thought man and beast together were a single
creature—in fact, a god. Horse riding soon took off
and the *charro*—a gentleman cowboy in dashing
traditional costume—became an institution.

The *charreada* is a Mexican-style rodeo where the *charros* get the chance to display their remarkable horsemanship. Women riders in bright costumes, singers, and musical bands combine to make this a colorful event. *Charreadas* are held regularly in Mexico City and on local ranches around the country. *Charros* also take part in special parades and horse shows.

The deep-rooted tradition of handicrafts expresses the Mexicans' natural artistry and love of color. The knowledge and techniques for producing pottery, wood carving, lacquerwork, textiles, and other crafts have been passed down through the generations in each region.

TRADITIONAL CRAFTS

The Spaniards helped the Indians to develop their trades, introducing new methods, designs, and skills. The combination of Indian and Spanish talents has resulted in a wide range of colorful high quality crafts, uniquely Mexican, available throughout the country (see next page).

For pure enjoyment Mexico offers every possibility. Major coastal resorts have yachts for hire and offer water sports from sailing, water skiing, para sailing, windsurfing, and surfing, to scuba diving and snorkeling. Deep-sea fishing is also popular along the Pacific coast of Baja California.

Mexico is fast becoming a popular golfing destination, with superb courses, some designed by top golfing names, all over the country. Some of the most magnificent courses are in Baja California, down the Pacific coast, and in Guadalajara, known as the golf capital of Mexico.

LEISURE TIME

HIGH FLYERS

Great drama is provided by the spectacle of the cliff divers in Acapulco. To watch the boys make their swan dive way down into a narrow cove, timing it to a split second to catch the swell of the wave, is always a thrill, and even more so at night when flares are lit at the moment of descent.

Equally dramatic is a performance by the Flying Men of Papantla, who perform an ancient Totonac ritual at Papantla, near Veracruz. One man plays a flute on a high platform, while four others spiral downwards upside down, spinning around the pole thirteen times before landing.

PYRAMIDS 58

CHURCHES 60

TO REFLECT 64

MODERN DESIGN 66

BOLD FAÇADES 72
FRENCH STYLE 74

COLONIAL 76

PYRAMIDS

The development of architecture in Mexico is divided into three distinct periods: Pre-Columbian, colonial, and modern. Its story can be traced back to the ancient Olmec people who created the earliest known monuments around the ninth century BC.

The Mayas, Teotihuacanos, Zapotecs, Mixtecs, Totonacs, Toltecs, and Aztecs are among the successive pre-Hispanic civilizations that went on to produce architectural forms of considerable significance. The first of the great builders were the Mayas, who developed an exquisitely refined style of architecture. Palenque and Bonampak, built in Chiapas around AD 700, are among the finest examples of their earliest pyramids and temples. Thanks to painstaking restoration works, many of these magnificent buildings can still be visited today.

The Spaniards brought their own designs with them and the delightful towns they built across the country contribute greatly towards Mexico's diverse architecture today. The Baroque style was originally from Spain, but was added to by Indian artists and took on a distinct Mexican flavor.

In the twentieth century dynamic young architects have produced an exciting blend of the ultramodern combined with influences from Mexico's pre-Colombian past.

Following the early constructions of the Olmecs, great pyramids and temples were built by successive civilizations as part of numerous ceremonial centers, dedicated to deities and paying tribute to the ruling priests. Buildings were highly colored and often covered with intricate carvings.

The Pyramid of the Niches at El Tajín (left) has an intriguing design. Some of the finest sites are the Mayan ruins of Chichén Itzá, Uxmal, and Palenque. El Castillo (the Castle), also known as the Pyramid of Kukulkán (above), at Chichén Itzá, is a majestic Maya-Toltec pyramid.

Once the conquest of the Aztec Empire had been accomplished the new Spanish rulers lost no time in starting to build. During their three hundred years of occupation they constructed hundreds of beautiful churches and monasteries—the churches dominating the main square in towns or villages.

CHURCHES

Although Spanish architects came to Mexico, Indian
artisans became increasingly involved in the work.
Religious architecture became the great art form of
this period, eventually flowering into these
colorful, carved facades, typical of Spanish baroque
styles influenced by Indian tradition and style.

A PLACE TO REFLECT

Spanish churches and monasteries have ornate, baroque interiors that are richly gilded, with every surface lavishly decorated. Outstanding among these are Santo Domingo in Oaxaca, the Church of Tepotzotlán near Mexico City, and the Chapel of the Rosary in Puebla's Church of Santo Domingo.

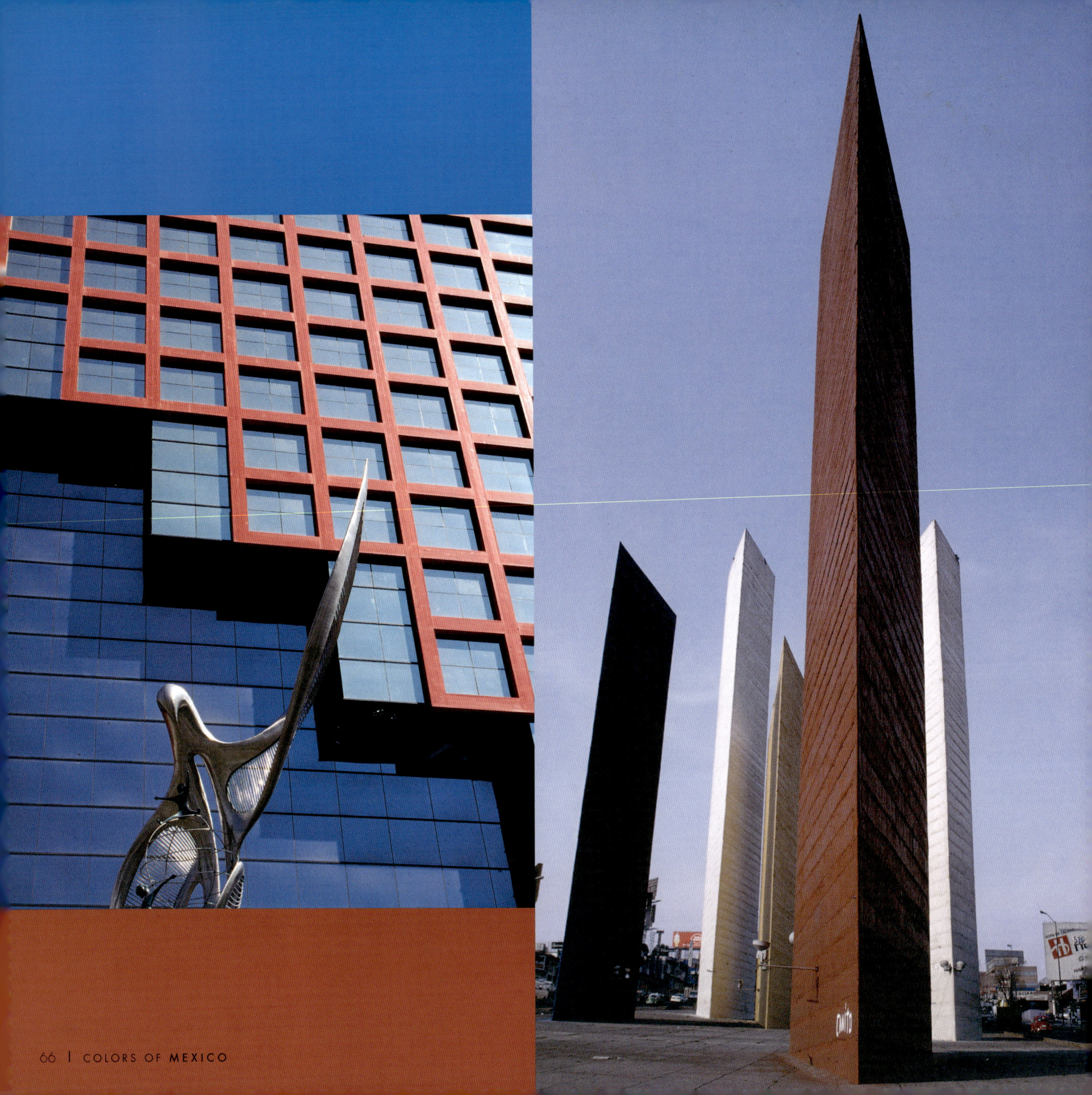

MODERN DESIGN

The early 1920s, post-Revolution, saw a fresh wave of architecture with the emergence of creative young architects who introduced entirely new concepts of contemporary Mexican design, using straight classical lines and vast areas of glass.

Bold and imaginative striking forms are often combined with pre-Hispanic themes. The use of space and vividly colored facades draws from Mexico's ancient roots. Mexico City's National Museum of Anthropology is an outstanding example of contemporary architecture, while the main buildings of University City are renowned for their stunning murals and mosaics.
Next page: The Cultural Center in Tijuana designed by Pedro Ramirez Vazquez.

BOLD FACADES

The Spanish were keen on using color to decorate their homes and you will find many streets in old colonial towns lined with houses painted white, blue, pink, yellow, and green. In Puebla, houses are typically decorated with brightly colored tiles. The use of local building materials has also produced varying color effects, seen in the mellow tones of elegant Morelia, the soft rosy hues of Taxco's beautiful Santa Prisca Church, and the pale green hues of Oaxaca's masonry.

This trend has been continued in modern hotels throughout the country, with exotic Mexican shades of hot pink, sapphire blue, terracotta red, and yellow ocher, adorning both exteriors and tastefully decorated interiors. Set in tropical surroundings, amid gardens of brilliant flowers and lush shrubs, many resort hotels present an enticingly colorful image.

FRENCH STYLE

The French-style colonial architecture of Santa Rosalia, in Baja California, is something of a surprise. The town was a French-occupied copper mining town in the 1870s and the clapboard houses lining the streets were built for workers with wood imported from the USA and Canada.

COLONIAL

Mexico's rich silver mines allowed the Spanish colonists to finance the development of fine new cities throughout the country. Guanajuato, Zacatecas, San Luis Potosi, and Taxco are among the major towns that grew up around the lucrative silver mines and are still flourishing today.

Other delightful towns include Morelia, San Miguel de Allende, Queretaro, Oaxaca, Puebla, and Merida. All feature typical Spanish characteristics— a central plaza surrounded by arcades, picturesque streets, and flower-filled balconies—but with distinct Mexican influences.

LANDMA
& VIEWS

LA BANDERA 80

MEXICO CITY 82

PILLARS & TEMPLES 86

VOLCANOES 88

DESERT CACTI 90

ROPICAL FLOWERS 92

LA BANDERA

One of Mexico's most exciting features is the drama and diversity of its landscape. In the northwestern region is Mexico's great natural wonder, the Copper Canyon. It is made up of a series of canyons, some even deeper than the Grand Canyon itself, that present an awesome panorama and a stark contrast to the expanses of cactus-strewn desert that form part of our familiar image of Mexico.

Among the most striking landmarks are the beautiful snow-capped volcanoes scattered across the elevated central plateau from east to west. The sight of the twin volcanoes of Popocatépetl and Ixtaccíhuatl, visible at times from high points in Mexico City, is always thrilling. Ancient ruins form a significant part of Mexico's landscape: the colossal Olmec heads; the great pyramids at Teotihuacán; the Atlantes (or warriors) of Tula, north of Mexico City; the hilltop center of Monte Albán; and the Mayan ruins hidden in the jungles and scrub forests of Chiapas and the Yucatan.

All over the country grand monuments glorify past heroes in Mexico's history. These include the much-loved statue of Cuauhtémoc, last Aztec Emperor, in Mexico City and colossal sculptures of Independence heroes—José María Morelos rising above Janitzio Island and El Pipilá towering over Guanajuato. Then there are the figures of revolutionaries Zapata and Pancho Villa, and former President Benito Juárez.

The story behind Mexico's flag relates back to its Aztec roots. While searching for a place in which to found their capital, so the legend goes, the wandering Aztecs saw an eagle on an island in Lake Texcoco, devouring a serpent on a cactus. Taking this as a sign from their god, they established Tenochtitlan there. The image of the eagle and the snake became the national emblem and is depicted on the Mexican flag.

The Mexican flag as it is today, was designed in 1821 in Iguala when the Plan de Iguala was issued, setting out the terms for Independence from Spain. In Mexico City's great square, the Zócalo, the flag is raised each morning with great pomp and ceremony and lowered again in the evening.

MEXICO CITY

Mexico's capital is the very pulse of the country, a driving force with a vitality and a dynamism that can be overwhelming at first. But to ignore it is to miss out on a vital aspect of Mexico. Built on the ashes of the former Aztec capital Tenochtitlán, it developed from a pleasant colonial city to the colossal metropolis of present day Mexico City, with one of the highest populations in the world.

Its elegant tree-lined boulevard Paseo de la Reforma, its grand Zócalo (right), Angel of Independence monument and the Latin American Tower, in addition to Chapultepec Castle and its

beautiful surrounding parklands, are all unique to
the city. Skyscrapers, deluxe hotels, lively
restaurants, along with the colonial ambience of its
historic center, street vendors, and markets are all
part of the scene of this vibrant and exciting city.
Next page: The rooftops of Guanajuato.

PILLARS & TEMPLES

Great pillars and columns were an important structural feature of many ancient temples. Standing on the base of a pyramid atop a hillside, four dramatic giant stone warriors known as the Atlantes (above), once supported the roof of a temple in the Toltec capital of Tula.

Other prominent groups of pillars constructed for functional purposes can be seen in Chichén Itzá in the Group of a Thousand Columns, and in Mitla, where the Hall of the Six Columns forms part of one of its most important complexes. The pyramid at Palenque is pictured right.

Mexico's spectacular snow-capped volcanoes are scattered among the central highlands. The highest is the perfectly shaped cone of Orizaba (Mountain of the Star). Best known are the "twin" volcanoes of Popocatépetl (the Smoking Mountain, above) and Ixtaccíhuatl (the White Woman), not least for the romantic legend woven around them. Popo, a warrior, fell in love with a chieftain's daughter. Believing he had been killed at war, she died of a broken heart. Upon his return, Popo laid her down on the mountain and kept guard over her in perpetuity with a burning torch. The volcano has

VOLCANOES

now become active again and is not visitable. The
other great volcano in the Puebla area is La
Malinche, named after Cortés's Indian mistress.
A cluster of volcanoes west of Mexico includes the
Volcán Nevado de Colima and Volcán de Fuego,
which has recently shown signs of activity.

DESERT CACTI

Baja California, where 60 percent of land is desert, is home to hundreds of varieties of cacti. Among the most striking are the towering *saguaros*, which can reach heights of up to sixty feet. Other species include several types of barrel cactus, the *nopal* (prickly pear) and the organ pipe.

Throughout the country you will be struck by the vibrant colors of Mexico's flowers, shrubs, and trees. In towns brilliant bursts of blossoms tumble from the balconies of the houses and you can glimpse bright, flower-filled courtyards.

TROPICAL FLOWERS

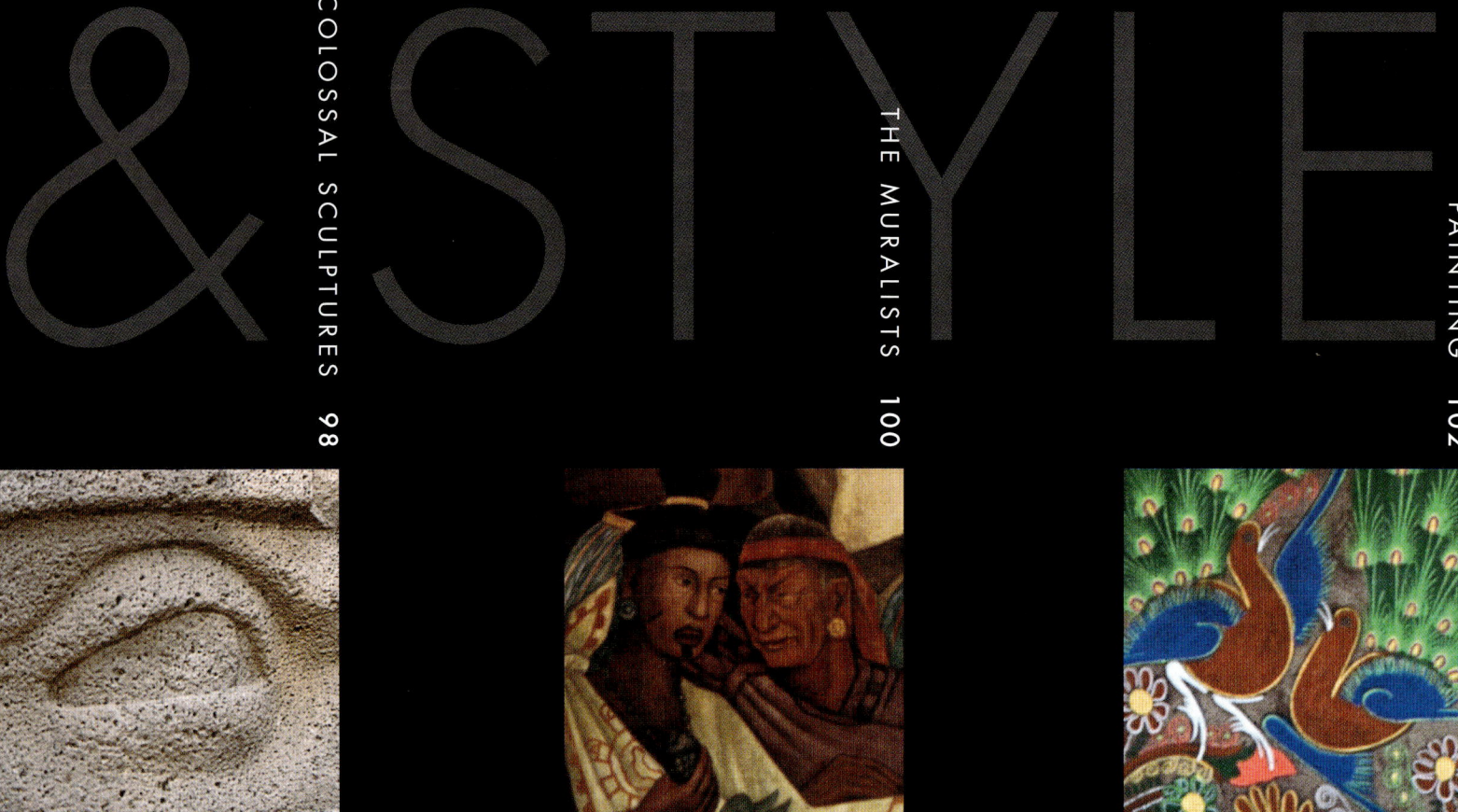

& STYLE

COLOSSAL SCULPTURES 98

THE MURALISTS 100

PAINTING 102

COLORS OF MEXICO: **ART, CULTURE & STYLE**

5

CARVINGS 104

ANCIENT RITUALS 106

MUSIC OF MEXICO 108

The enigmatic Olmecs, "people from the land of rubber," were the earliest known developed civilizations to emerge in pre-Hispanic times. Established around 1200 BC they made stone sculptures of animals, human forms, and deities.

COLOSSAL
SCULPTURES

Mexico has long been a creative and artistic nation. The art of fresco painting forming an important part of Mexico's culture. Frescoes and murals were used to decorate many pre-Columbian pyramids and temples, such as the Mayan frescoes in Bonampak. With the demise of the pre-Hispanic civilizations, art and culture in Mexico took on entirely new forms. While the Spaniards introduced their own styles of art and architecture, they recognized the artistic talents of the Indians, who were encouraged to decorate the interiors of churches and monasteries in their own way.

The late nineteenth century and early twentieth century saw the emergence of talented painters such as José Maria Velasco, José Guadalupe Posada, and Gerardo Murillo (or Dr Atl) who became known for his paintings of volcanoes. The aftermath of the Revolution also saw a renewed enthusiasm for murals and mosaics, with highly creative work produced by a new group of artists known as the muralists. Rufino Tamayo and Frida Kahlo, wife of muralist Diego Rivera, stand out for their outstanding contributions to the art world.

They are mostly identified, however, with the extraordinary carved colossal heads, characterized by helmets and Negroid features. Made from huge blocks of basalt they are thought to have been transported great distances on river rafts. Modern sculptors like to work on a large scale too (left).

THE MURALISTS

The muralist movement took off in the early 1920s, just after the Revolution had ended, when the walls of some public buildings were turned over to young artists of the time. The three most prominent mural painters to emerge were Diego Rivera, who had studied in Paris, Alfaro Siqueiros, and José Clemento Orozco. Their artistic development emerged from the social changes in Mexico and the new artistic trends in Europe. Rivera's murals are openly anti-capitalist, portraying the suppression of the Indian people.

One of his most striking works is the *History of Mexico*, a series of murals adorning the stairway in the National Palace. Outstanding works by Siquieros are the *March of Humanity* mural at the Polyforum and the National University mural. Much of Orozco's work can be seen in Guadalajara.

PAINTING

Mexicans have always favored the use of vibrant color to decorate their art forms. Pre-Hispanic peoples decorated sculptures of deities with brilliant adornments and gold masks. Nowhere is color more evident than in the handicrafts on sale in markets and stores. Brightly painted *amates* (bark paintings, left), pottery "Trees of Life", glazed ceramics, pâpier-maché figures and richly woven rugs and garments are all on display. Intense Mexican colors are also evident in modern paintings displayed by budding artists in Mexico City's parks.

CARVINGS

Ancient monuments were adorned with carvings to honor divinities. Recurring representations include jaguars and other animals, the rain god Tlaloc (known as Chac to the Maya), and the legendary plumed serpent Quetzalcóatl (Kukulkán in Mayan mythology). The serpent appears in various cultures, including those of the Toltecs at Tula and Chichén Itzá, Teotihuacán, Mitla and some Aztec pyramids. The Maya were accomplished stonemasons and fine examples of their exquisite work can be seen in Palenque and Yaxchilan, in southern Chiapas, where bas-relief carvings on lintels and stelae are a fascinating record of their lives and beliefs. Intricate carving and mosaic patterns adorning Mitla's palaces are a legacy of the craftsmanship of the Mixtec civilization.

Masks have been used since pre-Hispanic times in dances and ceremonies performed during religious festivals. They were often used for magical purposes, with the wearer taking on the form of a deity, a Catholic saint, jaguar, or other animal.

The tradition continues today in many regions, where fiestas combine ancient rituals with Christian influences. Masks are made from a variety of materials—wood, pâpier-maché or wax—and are often elaborately decorated to resemble animals, devils, or comic figures.

MUSIC OF MEXICO

Music forms part of everyday life in Mexico, in restaurants, bars, plazas, and parks. Unique to Mexico are the famed *mariachis*. Attired in their distinctive *charro* outfits with sombreros, these colorful roaming musicians sing about love and life, accompanied by string and brass instruments.

When it comes to folk music, each region has its own. Lively *jarocho* music is from Veracruz, while the introduction of an accordion gives an entirely different sound to *Norteña* music from the north. *Marimba* music of the south is gentler, and music of the Yucatan is known for its soft, romantic airs.

UNDERWATER WORLD 114

WATERFALLS 118

CAVERNS 120

NIGHTLIFE 124

NED GLASS 122

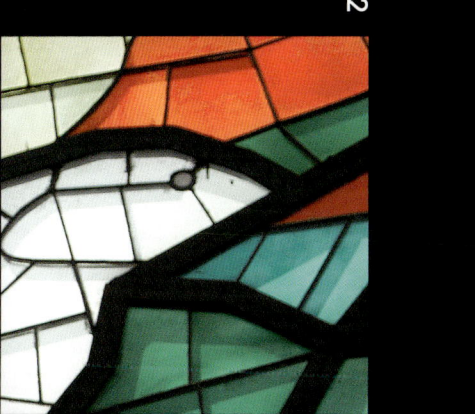

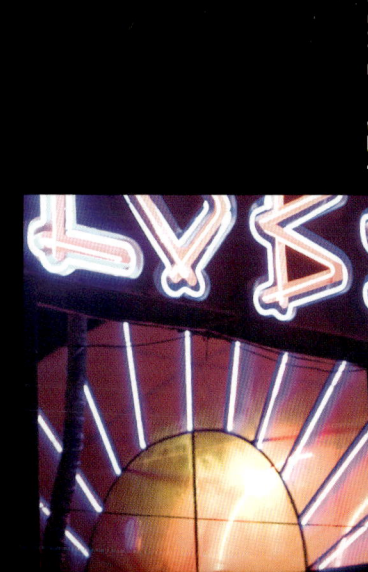

UNDERWATER
WORLD

Flying in to Mexico City at night your first sight will be a great burst of lights cast across the city like a net of brilliant jewels. By day you are more likely to notice the effect of pollution on the metropolis, but elsewhere in the country you will be struck by the transparency of the air and the clarity of the deep blue skies that cast a glow over the tropical blossoms, shrubs, and lush vegetation.

Unique to Mexico are the *cenotes* (natural limestone wells) dotted all over the Yucatan. These were sacred to the Mayas, who believed them to be the entrances to the spiritual underworld. Some are of exquisite beauty, revealing crystalline waters in brilliant shades of turquoise and emerald. The reflections of stalactites and stalacmites, combined with sunlight filtering through openings in the rocks and over translucent water creates an almost mystical effect.

With long coastlines bordering both the Pacific and the Caribbean Ocean, plus beautiful lagoons and *cenotes*, Mexico offers countless opportunities for snorkelling, scuba diving, and exploring marine life and underwater coral structures.
Next page: Danzante resort in Baja California.

WATERFALLS

Mexico has some spectacular waterfalls. Tucked away in the remote regions of the Copper Canyon, the Basaseachic waterfall has the longest single drop in the country. Rugged mountains surround the cascade as it plunges into an emerald pool.

Deep in the jungles of southern Chiapas, the
waterfalls of Agua Azul (above) present a
spectacular series of cascades in sparkling shades
of turquoise that tumble over rocks, forming pools
in which to swim.

The Yucatan is literally peppered with tunnels and caverns of natural rock formations where the Mayas would descend to communicate with their gods. The caves at Loltún contain murals painted by the Mayans.

CAVERNS

The Cacahuamilpa caves, northeast of Taxco, are full of stalagmites, stalagtites, and bizarre rock formations. Lighting has been installed to illuminate the fascinating forms, many of which are named according to the shape they resemble.

STAINED GLASS

The Mexicans' natural feel for color reaches a peak in stained-glass art forms. Vivid glass panels by Leopoldo Flores cover the walls and roof of the Art Nouveau conservatory in Toluca's botanical gardens (left). One window depicts a male figure amid flaming sun rays (above).

A modern stained-glass skylight by Salvador Pinoncelly is a prominent feature of the Museo Nacional de la Estampa in Mexico City. The convent of San Antonio in Izamal, Yucatan has a window with a religious theme (above).

Mexico's popular coastal resorts come to life at night. Big brash signs advertise countless discos and nightspots to enthusiasts, who can choose to dance the night away amid flashing lights or, more peacefully, under clear starlit skies.

Nights in Acapulco are nothing short of spectacular. As the sun goes down in a flaming Mexican sunset, Acapulco lights up. The bay shimmers with the reflection of a thousand lights and the resort glows with the lights of the restaurants which line Acapulco's main boulevard.

ON THE MOVE 130

COPPER CANYON 132

OPEN ROAD 134

DAWN & DUSK 136

SURFING THE WAVES 138

DIA DE LOS MUERTOS 142

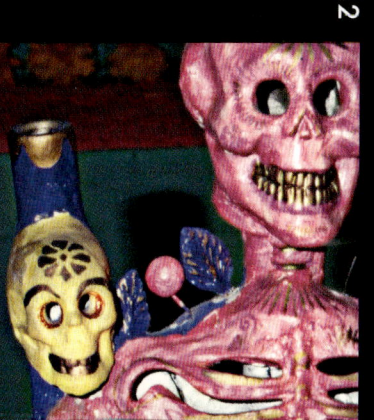

There's the Mexico of frantic pace and activity and then there's the other Mexico, a world apart, where the pattern of life is determined not by the clock, but by the rhythm of nature. In rural areas people have an entirely different concept of time. A local might remain squatting by the roadside for hours on end, waiting for a bus or for the unknown. You will see women sitting quietly all day selling their wares, often with a baby wrapped up neatly in a *rebozo*. You can come across a Tarahumara standing high up on a rockface gazing endlessly over far distant panoramas. The outlook on life is one of patience and acceptance.

In the big city it's all movement and energy. The Mexicans have a tremendous zest for life. With a tendency to live for the moment, they excel at enjoying themselves and making the most of things.

There are various ways of getting around Mexico's capital city. You can choose between buses, trolley-buses, and *peseros* (which operate fixed routes) or the metro. Taxis include Volkswagen Beetles, which cruise the streets, and *sitios*, which have fixed stands and offer better security.

Mexico has a well-run bus system. Operated by private companies, buses cover most of the country. For comfort, choose luxury and first class, which are equipped with air-conditioning, toilets, and monitors for video viewing. These buses generally travel on toll roads, with no unscheduled stops.

TO COPPER CANYON

For a unique railroad experience take the Chihuahua al Pacífico train though the Barranca del Cobre (Copper Canyon), one of Mexico's great natural wonders. The journey takes you through dramatic scenery, passing over countless bridges and through numerous tunnels

Stopovers give the opportunity to explore the wild and rugged surroundings and to descend into the canyons. You have the chance to meet Tarahumara Indians, who inhabit the region, and the Mennonites, who lead their own way of life in the area around Cuauhtémoc.

For a real feel of life in rural Mexico you can opt for adventurous travel on second-class regional buses. Serving small towns and villages, buses can be packed, not only with local people, but also with chickens, pigs, and other colorful passengers.

If you want the freedom to explore the country at your leisure, take your car. Mexico's network of roads ranges from modern *super carreteras* (four-lane tollways) and *cuota* (ordinary tollroads), to rolling *libre* (free roads) and regional roads, which can have ruts and potholes.

DAWN & DUSK

Watching the sun rise slowly from the ocean, turning the waters from pink to liquid gold, is a magical experience. The end of the day is just as beautiful. Gentle sunsets blur the outlines of the mountains in a soft haze while fiery sunsets light up the horizon in a blaze of hot Mexican colors.

SURFING THE WAVES

Surfing has taken off in a big way along Mexico's extensive coastline, down the Baja California peninsula, in Mazatlán, Huatulco, and other resorts along the mainland Pacific coast. Puerto Escondido in the southern state of Oaxaca is Mexico's surfing capital. Pacific rollers crashing on to its shores make for top-class surfing attracting enthusiasts from around the world.

Next page: Dusk in Mexico City's business district.

DIA DE LOS MUERTOS

In Mexico All Saints Day is known as Día de los Muertos (Day of the Dead). For weeks beforehand death is portrayed with flair, imagination, even humor. Shops and market stalls sell brightly colored skeletons, edible sugar skulls, and various other figures associated with death.

From sunset on November 1, people bring offerings of food and flowers to the gravesides of their loved ones and hold an all night wake in an atmosphere of peace and happiness.

CREDITS

The photographs used in this book are held in the Automobile Association's own photo library (**AA World Travel Library**) and were taken by the following photographers:

Peter Baker 31r, 95cl; **Fiona Dunlop** 120l; **Larry Dunmire** 5br, 11, 50bl, 74, 75, 80tr, 92tr, 98r, 110tl, 112bl, 114, 116/7, 127bl, 136, 137t, 137b, 138t; **Ken Paterson** 4bl, 31l; **Clive Sawyer** back cover center left, right, 3cl, 3r, 4br, 5bcr, 12/13, 14, 15, 18bl, 19bc, 20r, 21, 22, 22/3, 26bl, 26br, 27bl, 29, 30, 34bc, 34br, 35br, 38t, 38bl, 38/9, 39bc, 40, 41l, 41r, 42br, 43bl, 50tc, 52tl, 52tr, 52b, 53tr, 53b, 57bl, 57bc, 57br, 62l, 63, 65l, 67, 72l, 72r, 73, 76, 77, 78bc, 82l, 82r, 97bc, 97r, 106r, 108l, 109br, 113bl, 113bc, 122, 123r, 124tl, 124bl, 124br, 125, 126bl, 126bc, 127bc, 130, 131tr, 132, 138br, 139, 140/1; **Rick Strange** front cover, back cover left, center right, 3l, 3cr, 4bc, 5bcl, 5bl, 6, 8/9, 16/7, 18bc, 18br, 19bl, 20l, 24, 25r, 26t, 26bc, 27tl, 27r, 28, 32/3, 34bl, 35bl, 36, 37, 38bc, 39cr, 42tc, 42tr, 42bl, 43tl, 43tc, 43tr, 43br, 46l, 46r, 47, 48r, 49r, 50tl, 50tr, 50c, 50br, 51t, 51cl, 51c, 51cr, 51bc, 54l, 54r, 55l, 55r, 56bl, 56bc, 56br, 58, 58/9, 60l, 60r,

61l, 61r, 62r, 64, 65r, 66l, 66r, 70tl, 70bl, 70cr, 71tl, 71tc, 71cr, 71bl, 78bl, 78br, 79bl, 79bc, 79br, 80b, 81l, 81r, 83, 84/5, 86, 87, 88, 89, 90t, 90b, 91, 92l, 92br, 93, 94tc, 94tr, 94c, 94bl, 94br, 95tr, 95c, 95br, 96bl, 96bc, 96br, 97bl, 98l, 99l, 100, 101, 102, 103, 104b, 105, 106l, 107l, 107r, 108r, 109tl, 110tr, 110cr, 110bc, 111tl, 111bl, 111cr, 111br, 112bc, 112br, 115r, 118r, 119, 120r, 121, 126br, 127br, 128/9, 131tl, 131bl, 131br, 133, 134, 135, 138bl, 142, 143l, 143r, 144; **Steve Watkins** 71br; **Peter Wilson** 25l, 35bc, 42tl, 44/5, 48l, 68/9, 70bc, 99r, 104t, 109tr, 115l, 118l, 123l.